Raised Bed Gardening For Beginners:

How to Grow Plants and Vegetables in Raised Beds

By

Erin Morrow

Table of Contents

Introduction 5

Chapter 1. Benefits of Using a Raised Bed For Your Plants and Vegetables 7

Chapter 2. Best Plants and Vegetables Suited For Raised-Bed Gardening.. 10

Chapter 3. Materials Used in Raised Beds 13

Chapter 4. How to Build a Raised Bed 21

Chapter 5. Tips and Layout Suggestions 26

Conclusion 29

Thank You Page 30

Raised Bed Gardening For Beginners: How to Grow Plants and Vegetables in Raised Beds

By Erin Morrow

© Copyright 2015 Erin Morrow

Reproduction or translation of any part of this work beyond that permitted by section 107 or 108 of the 1976 United States Copyright Act without permission of the copyright owner is unlawful. Requests for permission or further information should be addressed to the author.

This publication is designed to provide accurate and authoritative information in regard to the subject matter covered. This work is sold with the understanding that the publisher is not engaged in rendering legal, accounting, or other professional services. If legal advice or other expert assistance is required, the services of a competent professional person should be sought.

First Published, 2015

Printed in the United States of America

Introduction

Have you recently taken up gardening as your hobby? Gardening is a very relaxing and helpful activity for any age, especially for those who have the "green thumb" or for someone who can grow anything. It has been proven a stress-reliever in most and a very lucrative venture in others who have decided to do gardening full time. At this time of age where people are getting more and more conscious of what they eat and getting more organic, what better time to start growing your own food?

One great technique in gardening is the one where the crops and the soil are raised and is called raised-bed gardening. Raised-bed gardening is a method of gardening in which the soil is formed in 3-4 foot wide beds which are usually made of wood, concrete blocks, or rock and may be accompanied with compost. It is found that those who use this method have higher chances of produce than regular or conventional row gardening. These plants are specifically spaced out so that the leaves are barely touching, leaving little room for weeds to grow and the use of compost greatly helps in its growth. These raised beds are recommended for the elderly because they would need to bend or exert themselves so much when gardening.

Chapter 1. Benefits of Using a Raised Bed For Your Plants and Vegetables

It is great for rocky, poor or abused soil or any other soil. You can customize the soil that goes in your raised bed.

It makes it easier and much more convenient for gardening every time. Since you do not need to strain too much in bending, these raised beds make it easier for you to plant, weed, water, and basically any gardening activity is done much easier and faster in these beds.

It is ideal for smaller spaces unlike conventional row gardening. You can do this kind of gardening everywhere; you just need to have an ample amount of space to out your beds in.

The deep rooting and better drainage capabilities of raised beds allows higher yields. You can expect to have more produce with these beds.

Since you may work the soil quicker in the spring in frost-hardened regions, it allows longer growing season.

It has good drainage and warmer soil in the early spring which allows more time for planting more vegetables.

Since it is raised, you do not have to walk on the soil to maintain your plants, which means it prevents soil compaction.

Raised beds require less watering because they have bigger soil volume as compared to containers.

Raised beds can be easily covered with netting or fleece so that the crops can be protected and at the same time, the cropping season is extended.

Raised beds save time and money. It saves you the hassle of digging and turning over your soil and you do not need to weed so much because when crops grow together, it's harder for weeds to grow with them as well.

Soil amendments and improvement efforts are concentrated in the raised beds and not in pathways which are covered with mulch or planted with low-growing cover crop or grass.

The way the bed's corners have rounded contours provide more actual growth in that area than the amount of flat ground.

All in all, raised beds improve the appearance of your garden and its accessibility because you can neatly place them in smaller areas as compared to a conventional row garden.

Chapter 2. Best Plants and Vegetables Suited For Raised-Bed Gardening

All kinds of plants and vegetables are suitable for raised-bed gardening and here are a few to guide you on what to plant in your raised beds.

Leafy green vegetables

These leafy greens such as spinach, kale, and lettuce are great for raised-bed gardening. Since raised beds warm quickly than the ground means that you can get several harvests with these crops because you can get started with them before summer even hits. The water in these beds quickly drains so these greens would not be soaked in so much water which they hate, that is why they are perfect for this type of gardening technique.

Onions

The reasons why onions are perfect raised-beds plants are because they hate soggy soil so the quick-draining soil in these beds is the perfect environment for them; onions also need plenty of organic matter, hence, the compost, and they also need a long growing season.

These onions may take up to 100 days to reach maturity, if they are grown from seeds so it best to grown these babies in places that have the four seasons because they need all the time they can get. Since raised beds warm up quickly, you can plant these onions early on for a longer growing time.

Root vegetables

Vegetables of this kind flourish in raised beds; these can be carrots, radishes, beets, and parsnips love soil with no rocks in them and a place where they have space to grow and spread out. If you want to grown plants with roots, it's very important to have complete control over the soil. With raised beds, you can customize the soil into your liking, making it rock, clay, and debris-free which might cause your roots not to grow.

Potatoes

Potatoes can grow anywhere but they are best for raised beds and they are much easier to harvest this way. They benefit from hilling the soil around the shoots as they mature and grow. Potatoes grown best when they are spread out and they thrive in loose and loamy soils that are easy to drain. With raised beds, you can control the composition of the soil and it is known that potatoes that were grown in raised beds have higher chances of produce than with other bigger tubers.

Tomatoes

Tomatoes need a soil which is nutrient-dense. With raised beds, you can control and customize your soil in any way so you can add more compost if you wanted to. Tomato cages and stakes are harder to stand and stay steady with loose soil though so this might be a bit of a difficulty in growing them in raised beds.

Chapter 3. Materials Used in Raised Beds

Probably one of the most important materials used in raised beds is the container which can be wood or concrete or other types of materials. To make sure the wood you use lasts, here are some tips:

Choosing thicker boards can make your wood last longer. A great example is using a teo0inch thick locally sourced larch must last 10 years even if there are no treatments done to it.

Regular pressure-treated lumber that are sold today have a mix of chemicals applied on it to prevent the moisture of the soil and weather from rotting it. Even though pressure-treated soil is considered harmless for organic growing, a number of people are still concerned of the various downsides in using it and prefer other eco-friendly alternatives.

More expensive woods such as cedar contain natural oils which prevent rotting and make them much more durable than other types of wood. They may be more expensive but they last longer in years.

Bricks or concrete blocks can also be used in these raised beds. The concrete, however, will boost the pH in soil over some time.

Railroad ties are not really recommended, especially the newer ties which use creosote-treated timber which is toxic. You might use very old ones if necessary.

Types of container materials and its Pros and Cons

You have a choice on what type of material to use in your raised beds, here are some that might give you ideas and listed are also the pros and cons to help you decide on what to get.

Wood

It is the most common material in making raised beds, and it probably the least expensive. Again, remember to use naturally rot-resistant woods like redwood or cedar and stay away from those that are preserved with toxins like creosote-soaked railroad ties. Woods that are still considered safe by the EPA are those that are pressure-treated with alkaline copper quaternary but you still might want to use weed barriers to line your beds to avoid the soil getting in contact with the wood.

Pros: Raised beds using wood are easy to install, and is readily available in most areas. They work nicely in either traditional or contemporary gardens which depend on the design and construction of the beds. It is one of the most cost-effective solutions for constructing raised beds and is perfect for those who are fond of DIY projects.

Cons: Wood cannot last forever; you will have to substitute them after sometime. However, untreated wood may actually last up to 10 years and treated wood will even last longer.

Concrete

It is now more widely used more for its aesthetic beauty or rustic designs than its functionality. There have been an increased use of concrete in landscapes and gardens over the years and some have started using them in their raised beds.

Pros: They last indefinitely especially when properly installed. They can be customized and suited according to your taste or even to match your house or other fixtures. They can work great with both traditional or conventional or even global gardening styles such as Spanish courtyards or Mexican stucco.

Cons: It is not really a project for DIYers out there and they can be expensive.

Rock

This is a simple DIY project for any gardener whether you are a beginner or an expert. You can use small boulders or large cobbles and they don't need to be mortared in place so they can still be replaced or changed. The raised beds can be curved or straight, depending on your preference and larger rocks can be pushed against one another and smaller ones placed together to make a border.

Pros: Rocks are widely available or can be found anywhere even in your backyard. You do not need any special equipment to install them and they can be customized and creatively lined for a cozier cottage-like look which any DIY homeowner can create.

Cons: These types of beds are not permanent and these stacked rocks may not work with any landscape style. Due to its mobility though, you can change and move your beds anywhere in your garden.

Cinderblock

Cinderblock can be used in several ways for your raised beds. They can be stacked to the desired height of the beds or they can also be permanently mortared in place and given a more elegant finish with a surface treatment and capped tops. The stacked ones appear more rustic and are inexpensive while the mortared ones can appear more elegant but has a higher price value.

Pros: Cinderblock is widely available and generally are very affordable. You can buy them at home improvement stores or supply stores for buildings. It is fairly durable and can stay in place for years and they can be creatively designed.

Cons: The pieces are heavy which requires more hands to make this bed.

Masonry

Masonry beds can easily fit any garden style, depending on the type of rock you will use. If you are a more experienced DIY person, you might be able to complete a task like this but most would use a masonry crew to complete this task.

Pros: Masonry materials are everywhere and can be easily found. They are very artistic and attractive and can blend in with other home fixtures or home exteriors.

Cons: It can be expensive, depending on the type of rick you will use.

Galvanized Culvert

Galvanized culverts are typically used for drainage for roadways but can make wonderful and stylish planters, when sliced and separated into sections, for a more contemporary garden.

Pros: They have a contemporary and cool look that are fairly available and are easily installed. They can easily be permanent fixtures in the garden and you will have more control over the size of your planter as compared to using stock tanks.

Cons: They are generally more expensive than stock ranks plus you will need to choose the size that would fit in your garden and have It cut in pieces which might incur additional cost. You would also need to have a truck or a means of transportation to transfer to your house or you might end up having it delivered, again at an additional cost.

Stock Ranks

Stock ranks are usually round or rectangular with rounded ends which are generally used to feed farm animals. These might be one of the easiest options for raised garden beds. You will need to add some drainage holes at the bottom of the stock ranks which can be easily done with drill.

Pros: Stock ranks are relatively affordable and readily available at feed stores. They are also known to alst indefinitely and there are no assembly requirements for this. They are highly movable and comes in various sizes so you could have variety in your garden.

Cons: You will need to hire a truck or have it delivered to your house at an additional cost and they might get really heated during the summer but still manageable.

Steel

Steel, specifically Cor-Ten is used for landscape projects and construction which can range from 3/16 or ¼ inch thick. Steel does give a rustic and old feel to your garden which can easily be combined with other house fixtures.

Pros: It gives a slim profile to your garden which can store more soil and plants. It's also one of the newer materials for raised beds so the aesthetic is up-to-date. It is less bulky and can withstand typical weather conditions which extend its life.

Cons: The material is generally heavy so you cannot install them by yourself. You will really need to have an expert or hire contractors to install them. Another downside is that it can deteriorate when you put it in a place or areas that receive salt spray from the ocean. It may not be the best choice for heat sensitive plants because steel adds heat to the soil. It is recommended to place steel raised beds in partly shaded areas so it won't get heated so much.

Chapter 4. How to Build a Raised Bed

There are few things to consider when you want to build raised beds for gardening. The first would probably be what kind material to use? If you chose wood, then what kind of wood would you use?

In most cases, cedar is the best choice for wooden raised beds because it is naturally rot resistant. Here are some good choices for cedar wood: Western red cedar, Vermont white cedar, Port Orford yellow cedar, Juniper, and Redwood. Redwood is limited to its resources but is also rot resistant. Generally, cedar beds can last up to 10 years or more, depending on the environment as well.

The next thing you should thing about is the height of your beds. You can build your beds up to 36 inches but the most common height is about 11 inches which is the height of two stacked 2"x6" boards. You can have beds as high as 6 inches only if you have good soil underneath the beds because the roots will go deeper to access more soil and nutrients. You can go higher of course but you have to consider the weight of the soil which will add pressure to the sides of the bed which might cause it to bow over and might spill at the sides. For these instances, it is recommended to use cross-supports in any beds that are higher than 18 inches or have a length more than 6 feet.

You might also want to consider the width of your bed. It is recommended that it be no wider than 4 inches because it is easier to reach across and you do not have to step on the bed itself just to plant something. This is ideal for normal sized people to people with long arms. It is better to have longer beds if your garden space allows it. It can be any length actually as long as the cross supports are set up every 4' by 6' alongside the length of the board.

Materials to be used:

Lumber/Wood:

It is recommended to use "2x" boards for the sides and these are commonly 2"x6" but you can also used 2"x4" or 2"x8" if it is the ones available. Use 4"x4" for the corer posts and cut 10" longer than the desired height of the bed. You will need extra posts to put in the middle of your beds are longer than 8". This is to prevent bowing and to provide support and secure the cross-supports.

Fastenings:

It is recommended to use 3.5" #10 coated deck screws for the beds. Six screws will be used for each corner and two for each mid-span post. If you will use cross-supports, use 1" stainless screws.

Cross Supports:

Get a few lengths of ½" aluminum flat stocks. You can get them in any hardware store and they are usually in 8' lengths.

Tools:

Mallet or sledge, hand saw, carpenter's level, square, screwdriver, drill, and a hacksaw.

Instructions:

Assemble and cut the basic frame and block it up to level. You will need to build the beds in place so clear the area of the construction. Use a square line the ends and saw the lumber to the preferred length. After that put two screws on each corner to hold them together. Set a level on the frame and use blocks to keep it level. Place them underneath. Do this for both ends and the sides.

Drive in corner posts and screw the boards into them. It is recommended to cut the pieces longer than what you will need and you can saw a point on the bottom of the posts if you like. Put the first post into the corner of the frame and push the post into the ground for a few inches. Using two screws per side screw the frame into the post. Set up the other posts and screw them in the same way.

Fill in the boards to ground and saw post tops flush to the sides. Then add the lower boards down to ground level by screwing them into the posts. You would have to fit the boards to the ground so you might need to dig in a bit to fit them. You can cut the sides where the boards stick up so that they are flush to the sides of the bed. Pat or step on the soil of the ground to smooth the pathway and start filling the bed with soil.

Putting cross-bracing. It is recommended to use cross-bracing if your beds are longer than 8' or taller than 18". This will secure the bed in place and prevent it from bowing from the sides. Use your hack saw to cut the aluminum flat stock. To secure, drill a hole in each end and use a 1" stainless screw to attach the brace to the posts, do this at either side of the span.

Put some soil on the bed and start gardening. Choose your best garden soil to put in the bed and is there are rocks, you can screen them through the piece of ½ mesh or pick up rocks you come across. Add other soils such as line, rock phosphate, peat, and organic fertilizer as needed. Spray some water into the soil and add more because the water will lower the soil level. Done and ready for planting!

Chapter 5. Tips and Layout Suggestions

Do a double-dig on the bed area. Turn over the soil and dig for at least 16" deep especially if the ground has never been used for gardening. Leave the soil piled up on the center of the bed and away from the sides so you can put the bed in place without obstructions. This digging will also give you a chance to pull rocks and see the composition of your soil.

Place the beds horizontally facing South. Place beds with the long side facing south because this will ensure equal light exposure for all the plants on the bed. If you do it the other way, the plants might not grow evenly because the taller plants out front may block the sunlight from the smaller ones at the back.

Level the beds. You will need a level to measure the soil. As you water the soil, it gets compressed and your soil level will decrease as a few weeks pass. You can use a kind of measurer like a stiff board about 2x4 and place it on top of the bed sides and set your level on this board. Be sure to check for level on both the length and across the width of your bed.

Inspect for roots. Check for roots as you dig around the soil. Pull out the root source because if you let it be, it will get the organic nutrients from the soil.

Spread out soil evenly. Add other soil amendments such as peat, lime pr compost and make sure to evenly spread out the soil. Water the bed with even spray and add more soil. Watering will settle the soil and lower it so you would need to add more soil on top of it. Use a rake to spread out the soil once more before planting.

Avoid stepping on the bed. Once you have prepared the soil and have started planting on it, do not step on it because it will compact the soil even more which will reduce aeration and impact the growth of the roots. Also, do not allow pets to play in the area because they will definitely step on the soil and even dig through it.

Mulch the pathways in between the beds. When you are buying mulch, make sure that there have been no issues about weed seeds in the mulch. Worth to mention that it is common for mulch from barks to have weed seeds which might sprout in your pathways. Regardless of them mulch though, some might continue to show up on your pathways. If this happens, wait till the moment it rains before pulling out the weeds. The weeds tend to come out easier if the ground is wet.

Leave a big gap between the beds and the pathways. You can use a wheelbarrow to measure the width between the pathways and he beds themselves. This gives you room to move around while you are gardening and also avoid people walking through from bumping into the beds and pulling out the plants.

How to avoid burrowing pests. If you have burrowing pests like moles, you can lay a layer of galvanized mesh or hardware cloth of about ½ to ¼ inches. The mesh should be stapled in place and continue upwards to about 3 inches more along the insides of the bed. You might want to put the mesh lower in the ground by digging deeper once you set up the bed, that is of you plan to grow root crops like carrots or potatoes. These techniques will keep your burrowing pets, like cats, rabbits, and other pests or critters, away from your garden and leave your crops to grow in peace.

Conclusion

There you go! These are the essential things you need to know of you are a beginner in the gardening world. It is not so easy to plant vegetables or any kind of crop without the proper instructions and basic materials. For this project, you were given information about raised beds which are popular nowadays because of it yielding more produce than the conventional row planting and its space-saving qualities.

There are more methods, ways, and techniques in gardening and you will eventually learn them as you go on with your gardening adventure. Just remember that plants need plenty of sunlight, water or for some plants, just enough water, a place or a garden to grown in and thrive and of course, a loving and caring hand to grow them. Gardening actually cultivates patience and gives you a peaceful time to meditate and concentrate on simple things such as planting and watching them grow.

Thank You Page

I want to personally thank you for reading my book. I hope you found information in this book useful and I would be very grateful if you could leave your honest review about this book. I certainly want to thank you in advance for doing this.

If you have the time, you can check my other books too.

www.ingramcontent.com/pod-product-compliance
Lightning Source LLC
LaVergne TN
LVHW021747060526
838200LV00052B/3522